First published in the United Kingdom in 2020 by Triangle Publishing Ltd Eventus Business Centre Sunderland Road Market Deeping PE6 8FD

ISBN 9781838212407

This book can be ordered from the publisher at **www.theactivemag.com** or try your local bookshop.

We have taken every care to ensure these walks are up-to-date and accurate at the time of publication. If you notice any changes or errors, please let us know by email to **walks@theactivemag.com** We will endeavour to update the information for the next printing of the book.

The maps in this guide are for illustration only and you should take your own OS map or a navigation device on all walks.

Author
Will Hetherington

Design
Matt Tarrant

Publishers
Triangle Publishing Ltd

CW00376827

Foreword

'It's a truth universally acknowledged that a good walk should end at a pub. Preferably one that accepts dogs,' to terribly misquote Jane Austen, but a pretty good sentiment anyway.

When talking to readers of Active magazine we often get asked when we are going to do a book of Will's Walks. So we've listened and got together with Will to bring this book to you. He's always out and about with his dogs around Stamford and Rutland and now we can all explore the area with him.

Unlike Will I am not from Stamford, but as a blow-in of well over 30 years I feel I can claim squatter's rights now; it's home with a capital H. Stamford and Rutland is an area I love and feel great attachment to, and enjoy being part of its friendly community. It's a beautiful part of the country with fabulous scenery and excellent walking, with the odd hill thrown in to get the heart rate up.

Midge, my lurcher, and I are obviously out and about daily, come wind or rain but sometimes it's nice to go somewhere different than the usual romp across the local fields. This book offers inspiration as well as opening up nooks and crannies in the area that I knew nothing about. I do now and am going to greatly enjoy exploring them. I hope you do too.

Mary Bremner - Active Magazine Editor

Active magazine, your local healthy lifestyle magazine

Inspiring people to stay healthy and enjoy a fulfilling life is the purpose behind our pages every month. We say, get off the sofa and get going!

Active is packed full of well written, interesting editorial including local features, fascinating people, health advice, local news and sport, cycle routes and, of course, walks. The magazine covers the Welland Valley including the towns of Stamford, Oakham, Uppingham, Market Harborough and Oundle, and all surrounding villages. Pick up your copy locally in supermarkets or one of our many local businesses.

Find us online at www.theactivemag.com

Facebook
theACTIVEmag

Twitter
@theACTIVEmag

Instagram
theactivemaguk

'There is an almost unsung quality about the variety of walking in this area'

I was born and bred in Stamford and still live in this marvellous town. I love the area just as much today as I always have. Over the years I have walked most of the footpaths in Rutland and the Stamford area and I revisit my favourites regularly. Not least because I have two labradors who, regardless of weather conditions, always want a walk.

There is an almost unsung quality about the variety of walking in this area. There are days in the hills of Rutland when the sun is shining and the lambs are bleating when it feels and sounds like a gentler version of the Yorkshire Dales. But if you go east of Stamford, no more than five miles, the hills fade into the flatness of the Fenland edge, which provides a fascinating backdrop to some of the walks in this guide. But overall I think gentle is the right word for walking in these parts. Nowhere does the land rise much more than 200 metres above sea level and one is never more than three miles from a village. But equally there is a remoteness to some of the paths, which allows that sense of adventure and departure from the madding crowd, which can be so rewarding when walking.

With limestone, sandstone or ironstone the predominant building material in the ancient villages of the Welland valley area there's no end of beautiful churches, rectories, quaint cottages and manor houses to drool over. And the likes of Burghley House, the Harringworth viaduct and Rutland Water make for important landmarks and significant attractions.

In this guide you will find a selection of some of my favourite walks around the area, which have been published in Active magazine over the years. This wonderful magazine is and always has been run by people who live in the area and they care passionately about everything that happens here. I think that is evident in the end result.

The walks in this guide are split into three categories: one hour maximum, between one and two hours, and two hours plus. We did this because the best walks don't always have to take hours and hours, and sometimes we have more time. But hopefully you will find a few new ones and some reassuring old favourites. My only advice is to take a map or download the OS App. You never know when you might need it. Oh and if a walk takes longer or less time than I have suggested then remember we all walk at different speeds and have different levels of vulnerability to distraction along the way.

Do I have a favourite? Well, there's a tricky question in such a beautiful area, but I suppose I would choose the walk I do the most, which is in this guide naturally. It's from Stamford town meadows along the river Welland all the way to Tinwell, up the hill to Easton and then back past the ruins at Wothorpe into Stamford. It's six miles door to door for me, which is perfect for a weekend walk and the dogs love it even more than I do.

I really hope you enjoy this compendium of local walks and it helps to provide a bit of inspiration when you are looking for somewhere new. I might see you out there.

Happy Walking!

Will Hetherington - Author

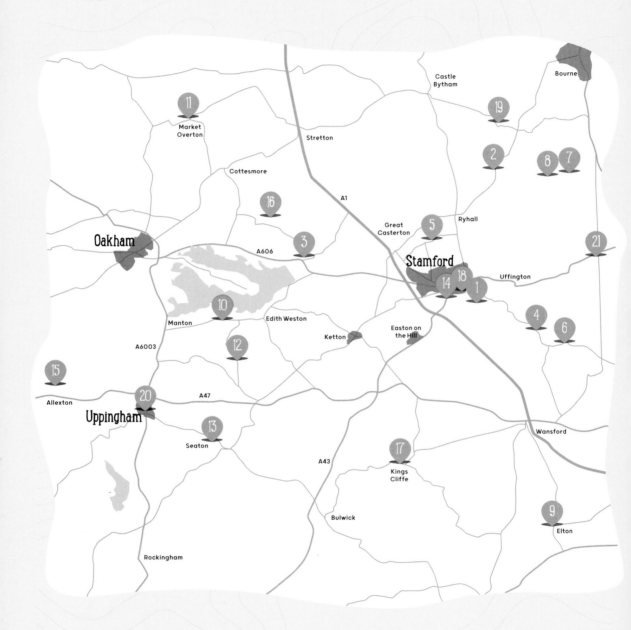

Contents

ROUTE MAP KEY

 Start/finish   Walk route   Direction   Village / Town   Woodland

Road   River/lake/reservoir   Railway   Church   PH Public House

1 HOUR WALKS

I work from home but even
then I sometimes find it hard
to get away from the house
for much more than an hour,
but luckily there are plenty of
great shorter walks around
to provide some variety.

1. Burghley Park

We are lucky to have access to the treasures contained within Capability Brown's wonderful parkland, not to mention Burghley House itself

THE ROUTE

There are many different ways to enjoy Burghley Park but my favourite is to walk in via the Station Gate at the junction of Water Street and Barnack Road. This route takes you past the well established Princess Diana Memorial Garden and Burghley Park Cricket Club on the right. As you approach the house along the mile long drive you can fully appreciate the majesty of the park with its ancient trees. If you want to make a loop bear left 300 metres before the house to walk down Queen Elizabeth's Avenue and turn right at the bottom to approach via the stables.

These trees were originally planted in avenues in the 17th century under the instruction of the fifth Earl of Exeter. However in the late 18th century the ninth Earl brought in Capability Brown, the most famous landscape gardener of them all, to shake things up. He created the Serpentine Lake and removed a lot of the original lime avenues, setting out the park as it remains today, using mainly English oaks. On a hot summer's day these broad-leaf trees offer vast areas of welcome shade to visitors and of course the resident herd of fallow deer, who are so used to visitors you can almost touch them.

When you get up to the house you can pop into the orangery for lunch or a drink, or enjoy a picnic on the lawns in front of the house. Afterwards follow the ha-ha round, taking in the views of the house, the ancient large-leaved lime and the massive oriental plane in the same area. When you get to the Serpentine Lake go past the Lion Bridge and then make your way west and out of the park. There is tremendous freedom to roam the parkland and you will never be cramped for space. To enjoy a full loop leave the park via the Bottle Lodges and stroll back into Stamford down magnificent St. Martin's.

The house and gardens

The house was built by William Cecil, Lord High Treasurer to Queen Elizabeth I, between 1555 and 1587, and is open to visitors. If you want to go straight there drive east from Stamford for one mile down Barnack Road and turn right into the visitor entrance at Pilsgate Lodges. From here you can spend the day exploring the Garden of Surprises and the Sculpture Garden. The south gardens are also open at selected times of year for special events. For more information about prices and opening times visit www.burghley.co.uk

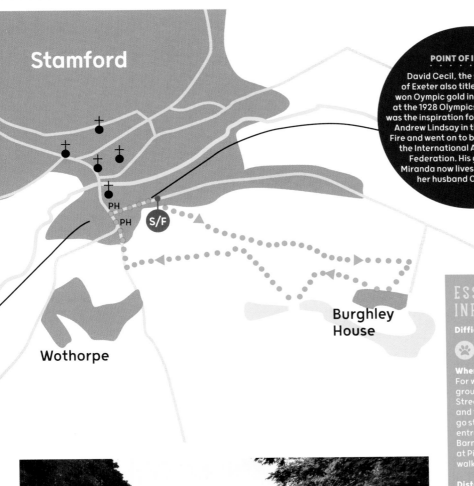

Stamford

PH

PH

S/F

Wothorpe

Burghley House

POINT OF INTEREST

David Cecil, the sixth Marquess of Exeter also titled Lord Burghley, won Oympic gold in the 400m hurdles at the 1928 Olympics in Amsterdam. He was the inspiration for the character Lord Andrew Lindsay in the film Chariots of Fire and went on to become president of the International Amateur Athletics Federation. His granddaughter Miranda now lives in the house with her husband Orlando Rock.

ESSENTIAL INFORMATION

Difficulty rating

Where to park
For walking in the whole grounds park on Water Street or Barnack Road and for visitor attractions go straight to the visitors' entrance a mile down Barnack Road and enter at Pilsgate Lodges. Or just walk in from Stamford.

Distance and time
If you walk in and out of the park from Stamford it's about three miles in total and will take an hour if you don't stop. But if you take a picnic then relax and enjoy a whole day.

Highlights
Space, the views of Stamford, the magnificent house, ancient trees, Lion Bridge and the Bottle Lodges.

The pooch perspective
This is not a great place for dogs as they are not allowed off the lead in the wider park because of sheep and there are deer within the inner fenced parkland.

Tallington 188
049138

2. Carlby and the West Glen river

This is a perfect short summer stroll which your dogs will love

THE ROUTE

There is space for three cars right by the church gate on Church Street in Carlby and it's best to tuck your car in as tight as possible here.

From here walk straight through the churchyard, and then turn left when you come out of the gate at the other side. Turn right just by the beautiful entrance to the Old Rectory and into The Paddocks. The path goes down to the left of the houses here and quickly brings you out on the banks of the West Glen river where you will shortly find a couple of strategically placed benches if you want to sit and watch the clear water gently gurgling by. It's a perfect little spot with lots of shade for a summer's day.

Follow the path and then turn left over the bridge and take the obvious footpath which leaves the river to head

up to Essendine and Broadholme Farm. Follow the path through the farm and when you get to the road on a corner, with a grand old house right in front of you, turn right and follow the road around. You will soon have woodland on your right, but keep going on the track until you can go no further at the bottom with the East Coast mainline blocking the way.

Turn right here and on to the permissive footpath which follows the western edge of the field until you reach the West Glen river again. Turn right at the river and follow the track until you get back to the bridge you crossed at the start. Cross the bridge but don't turn right to retrace your steps, because there's a good path between two hedgerows which goes all the way back up to Church Street.

ESSENTIAL INFORMATION

Difficulty rating

It's a short one with no stiles so it's as easy as they get.

Where to park
There's space for three cars just by the church gate on Church Street in Carlby or on the main road in the village.

Distance and time
Two and a half miles/ one hour.

Highlights
St Stephen's church in Carlby. The clear waters of the West Glen river. An extremely peaceful walking area thanks to the permissive footpaths.

The pooch perspective
The dogs will love the West Glen and there's no livestock here.

Carlby

S/F

Essendine

POINT OF INTEREST

The West Glen river has a number of sources near to Old Somerby and Boothby Pagnall and it passes through Bitchfield and Corby Glen before reaching Carlby and Essendine. It then flows to Greatford before joining the East Glen river at Wilsthorpe and becoming the River Glen, which feeds the Welland at Surfleet Seas End.

948 086
Rutland.

3. Empingham village

This short stroll in the heart of Rutland is rewarding in more ways than one

THE ROUTE

You can park near the main crossroads in the middle of Empingham. Walk up Exton Road and the footpath runs east from opposite the cricket club car park. The path starts out across the southern edge of some large fields with the village down to the right. You soon come to a gateway on the right hand side, which leads to Loves Lane.

Cross the tarmac road and carry on over the stile on the other side of the road before dropping down over some more arable fields, and then over another stile into a grassy meadow with some wetland and reeds in it. The next gateway brings you into the bottom end of Gunnel Lane, a small cluster of old houses at the very bottom of the village on its eastern edge. Follow the track up to the road and turn left to head out of the village.

Turn right on to Mill Lane and follow the road down to the cattle grid and then skirt around the left of the old farmhouse ahead of you. After the farmhouse head for the steel bridge over the Gwash. This modern bridge lacks rural charm but it's certainly not going to fall into the river any time soon. There is also a brand new cattle crossing here which is a very useful place for your dogs to take a dip in the river.

After the bridge turn left and follow the path round the edge of the field until you see it cutting straight across the field to the right. Take this right turn and you are now heading back towards the village over a couple of fields and around the top of the belt of woodland surrounding the Gwash on your right. Before long you will arrive back at the main road into Empingham. Turn right and head back up the hill into the village with the church on your right.

Empingham

PH

S/F

POINT OF INTEREST

The river Gwash was dammed up at Empingham to create Rutland Water in 1976, but the Gwash still resumes its course from here today and meanders around eastern Rutland before joining the Welland to the east of Stamford near Hudds Mill.

A606

ESSENTIAL INFORMATION

Difficulty rating

It's not flat otherwise it would be one paw!

Where to park:
You can park anywhere near the main crossroads in the middle of Empingham.

Distance and time:
Two miles; a leisurely 45 minutes.

Highlights
Some lovely views at the start of the walk and a pleasing blend of countryside and village life.

The pooch perspective
There might be some cattle in a field or two but not when I have been there. On a hot day the dogs can get into the Gwash to cool off near the end.

4. Hills and Holes and Walcot Hall

An old limestone quarry and a glimpse of grandeur make this an interesting loop

THE ROUTE

You can park in any one of the convenient parking areas around the edge of the intriguing 50-acre Hills and Holes nature reserve in Barnack. Once you have entered this Site of Special Scientific Interest enjoy a stroll around the deep hollows and let the children play hide and seek. But be careful not to damage any of the 'flora, fauna, or geographical features' or you may be hit with a £20,000 fine by Natural England!

When you are ready to start Phase Two of this walk (probably after about 15 minutes) make your way to the southwest corner of the site along any of the multitude of tracks. Look for the footpath which runs beside the high stone wall away from the village. This will take you along a field boundary until you pop out on to the road on a right angle bend. Turn left here and join the Hereward Way. Go through the gateway and into the pastures in front of Walcot Hall. Keeping the high wall on your left pass the grand gates which provide a majestic view of the Hall and keep going. It's a peaceful landscape away from any traffic and it's also easy walking on well defined tracks.

079 043
Tally map.

The path makes a very gradual descent towards the village of Southorpe as you pass through a couple of fields, before eventually joining the road in Southorpe at Grange Farm.

Turn left and walk north along the road through the village. You have to walk on the road for a small section of this, but it shouldn't be too busy. Look out for Southorpe Meadow on the right. This is a wildflower-rich hay meadow which features some rare flowers in spring and summer and is also a Site of Special Scientific Interest.

And on the left of the road is a large piece of limestone, which has been there since Peterborough and Ely cathedrals were built circa 1450. According to the plaque on the stone it fell off one of the carts transporting it from the quarry to the River Nene.

When you reach a sharp right hand turn in the road at the northern edge of Southorpe look for the stile next to Hall Farm. Cross over here and go through the grassy meadow and the arable field towards Barnack. Cross the road after the arable field and re-enter Barnack on the footpath by the cricket club where you can either turn left or carry on and explore the village.

ESSENTIAL INFORMATION

Difficulty rating

Where to park
There are a number of parking areas around the Hills and Holes in Barnack.

Distance and time
Three miles/one hour.

Highlights
The Hills and Holes (often referred to as hollows) is a special place which acts as a giant playground. The walk past Walcot Hall is peaceful and the view of the house which was built in the mid 17th century offers a glimpse of a life less ordinary.

The pooch perspective
Keep the dogs under control in the Hills and Holes and be respectful of the signage around Walcot Hall. There's not really any fresh water on the way round so even though it's not far be careful on a hot day.

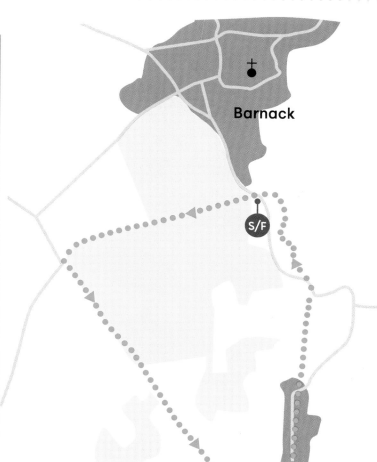

Barnack

S/F

Southorpe

POINT OF INTEREST

Barnack Hills and Holes is a grassland area which has developed on the site of disused quarry workings. The Lincolnshire limestone quarried here was used in the construction of many of the local village houses and nearby Peterborough Cathedral.

5. Little Casterton and Tolethorpe

A picturesque walk with a hint of Shakespeare and plenty of water

THE ROUTE

Park in Little Casterton on the main road as close to Church Lane as you can. Walk down the lane until you get to the footpath on the right just before The Chantry, a rather grand looking country residence. Follow the path down past the quiet and secluded church on the left. In fact if you didn't take this path you would be hard pressed to know there was a church in Little Casterton.

You will soon find yourself crossing the outfield of Tolethorpe Cricket Club, with its quaint pavilion, and then onwards into the sheep pasture field in the grounds below Tolethorpe Hall. Follow the path to the north eastern corner of this field and the wall around the back of Tolethorpe Hall, famous home of the Stamford Shakespeare Company.

Go through the gate here and follow the track around the side of Tolethorpe Mill and along the drive on the other side of this beautiful country home. When you reach the end of the drive with the bridge on your left, you can turn left and take a quick right to walk along the side of the Gwash but it's a bit limited. It's far better to turn right and walk up the road until you get to the gateway at the top. Go through the kissing gate and then over the stile and take a sharp left and carry on all the way down the hill (ignoring the footpath to the right almost immediately). This is a permissive footpath which follows the horseshoe of the Gwash here and gives the dogs ample opportunities to dip in and out on those hot summer days.

Once you have gone all the way around the horseshoe and are facing south again you will see the path heading west and upwards across the middle of the field. When you reach the top it's a simple case of retracing your steps back to Little Casterton.

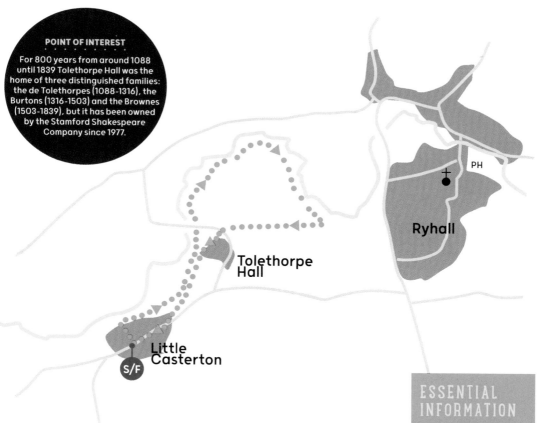

POINT OF INTEREST

For 800 years from around 1088 until 1839 Tolethorpe Hall was the home of three distinguished families: the de Tolethorpes (1088-1316), the Burtons (1316-1503) and the Brownes (1503-1839), but it has been owned by the Stamford Shakespeare Company since 1977.

PH

Ryhall

Tolethorpe Hall

Little Casterton

S/F

ESSENTIAL INFORMATION

Difficulty rating

It's a decent walk but nothing too taxing.

Where to park
On the main road in Little Casterton as close to Church Lane as possible.

Distance and time
Two and a half miles and one hour maximum.

Highlights
The church and cricket club in Little Casterton, Tolethorpe Mill and the River Gwash.

The pooch perspective:
The presence of the Gwash all the way around the horseshoe makes this a firm favourite with the dogs. Otherwise watch out for the sheep.

095041

Tally Map

6. Ufford and Barnack

One of England's finest churches and two charming villages make this a perennial favourite

THE ROUTE

I parked on Main Street in Ufford near The White Hart pub. From here walk west along Walcot Road away from the pub. You will have the church on your left, and when you get to the end of the high stone wall on your right turn right into the entrance to Ufford Park Cricket Club. When you reach the large new house on its own take the footpath to the left of the house and follow this gradually downhill. Stick to the path as it makes a few right angle turns around the edge of a large arable field, passing a strategically placed bench in a corner along the way. From here you can see the rather grand Walcot Hall to the west. The path goes down the south side of Ufford Oaks, a well-established block of woodland, before joining a larger farm track/footpath running north/south at the bottom. Turn right here and stay on the track for 500 metres until you reach the left turn towards Barnack. But make sure you look

back and enjoy the view of Ufford.

Follow the path into Barnack and turn right when you reach the edge of the village. This path will bring you out on Main Street right by the impressive church in the village. Turn right here and follow Main Street around until it reaches the B1443, the main road running through the village. Turn right again and follow the road out of the village. When you leave Barnack you will very shortly come to the Torpel Way footpath leading off into the fields to the right.

Take this path and follow it round as it takes you to The Synhams wood via a small wooden bridge. Go through the wood and keep going straight along the northern edge of the next field until you get to the field boundary. Turn right here and follow the path until you reach the road back to Ufford. Walk along the road and up the very gradual incline back to your car.

ESSENTIAL INFORMATION

Difficulty rating

There are no hills to speak of and very few stiles, and it's pretty easy underfoot.

Where to park
On Main Street in Ufford near The White Hart pub.

Distance and time
Three and a quarter miles/one hour (at a good pace).

Highlights
There are a number of good views of Barnack and Ufford and Walcot hall from the path between the two villages. Barnack church and the White Hart in Ufford have their own strong but differing attractions...

The pooch perspective
This is mostly arable land so there's not much livestock around. There's limited water but it's not a long walk so that shouldn't be too much of a problem.

POINT OF INTEREST

The website greatenglishchurches.co.uk describes St. John the Baptist church in Barnack with its superb Saxon tower as one of "England's finest churches". It elaborates: "Barnack is one of those few churches where just about everything within or without is either unique or exceptionally fine."

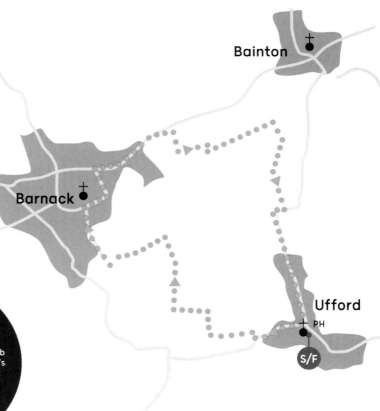

Bainton

Barnack

Ufford
PH

S/F

091 138
Tally map

7. Wilsthorpe and Braceborough

Relax in the tranquillity provided by this rural backwater, and enjoy a skyline dominated by an impressive church spire

THE ROUTE

I parked on the road right by the church in Wilsthorpe but you can also choose to start and finish in Braceborough if you prefer. The public footpath heads south west out of Wilsthorpe from opposite the church. Initially you walk down a wide gravel drive then over a couple of small grass fields before reaching the arable land beyond, with the Manor House over to your left. Go under the power lines and you will soon come to the metal bridge over the East Glen river. The bridge crosses the river just 400 yards west of the point where it joins forces with the West Glen River.

Cross the bridge and keep heading south across a big field, then go through the hedgerow and turn right. Stay on the path as it goes around a small spinney and then after 100 yards or so turn right and cross over the new wooden bridge through the gap in the hedge. (If you have the time and the inclination you can make a short detour to Greatford at this point and then retrace your steps).

From here head north across one big arable field and then one smaller ridge and furrow type wild meadow with two or three lovely trees in the field edges. You will arrive in Braceborough on the village green (for want of a better description) and see the church and Braceborough Hall Nursing Home straight ahead. It's worth a stroll around the peaceful little place but to follow the route you need to turn right as soon as you get into the village. Follow the path through a farmyard then out on to the fields on a well established road. From the edge of the village it's less than one kilometre back to the metal bridge over the East Glen and Wilsthorpe beyond.

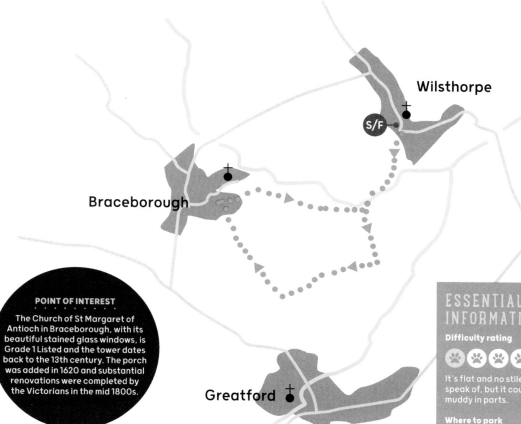

Wilsthorpe

S/F

Braceborough

Greatford

POINT OF INTEREST

The Church of St Margaret of Antioch in Braceborough, with its beautiful stained glass windows, is Grade 1 Listed and the tower dates back to the 13th century. The porch was added in 1620 and substantial renovations were completed by the Victorians in the mid 1800s.

ESSENTIAL INFORMATION

Difficulty rating

It's flat and no stiles to speak of, but it could be muddy in parts.

Where to park
I parked right outside the church in Wilsthorpe but you can start and finish in Braceborough if you would prefer.

Distance and time
Two and a quarter miles/50 minutes. You can extend the walk into Greatford if you wish.

Highlights
Braceborough church is an impressive sight from the east and there is a soothing tranquility about the whole walk. Nothing happens very fast in either of these two villages.

The pooch perspective
I didn't see any livestock when I did it and the East Glen provides a handy spot for a drink and cool off if the dogs can negotiate the bank.

Troubleshooting tips for walkers

How to take good care of yourself when walking, by Liz Clare from Cell Regeneration

Taking a stroll outside and breathing clean air is good for the soul, and it's also a fantastic form of exercise for people of all ages and abilities. But if you're going to do something you might as well do it right.

Here are a few tips to help you stay safe when out and about:

Warm up
Always start slowly, make sure you do some gentle warm up exercises to wake up the muscles and get the blood flowing. Warm ups are one of the most effective ways to reduce the risk of injury.

Build up gradually
If you're not used to walking regularly then start with some shorter walks and gradually build up to the longer and more challenging walks. Your body will thank you for it.

Stay hydrated
Drinking water before, during and after your walk is essential.

Use the right technique
Always stand as straight as you can and walk at a steady, manageable pace with your arms swinging freely by your side. Each step should be a rolling action from heel to toe.

Get the right gear
Wear thick, comfortable and breathable cotton socks inside sensible, durable and supportive lightweight shoes.

Cool down
If you warm up, you have to cool down. Just a few stretching exercises will suffice, and it's a great way to stave off muscle soreness.

If you suffer from osteoarthritis, osteoporosis, long term or recurring issues then please contact our experienced and friendly health professionals for advice. The award winning MBST technology is also available in Tinwell just outside of Stamford in Rutland. As a company we promote people being active and it is our ethos to keep people doing what they love. This is why we are honoured to present this wonderful walking guide with Active magazine. We hope you enjoy your walks pain free.

Five common walking injuries

Walking is a safe and low-impact form of exercise, but injuries can still occur.
This often happens when you suddenly increase the distance and difficulty of your walks.
Here are five common walking problems and how to treat them.

1 Lower back strain

Tight hamstrings and a weak core are normally the cause of lower back strain as well as not carrying, lifting or twisting correctly. The best way to rest the back is to literally lie down. But after a few days of rest after the injury start stretching your hamstrings a few times per day to improve your flexibility and relieve tension in the lower back. The second step is to strengthen the muscles that stabilise the spine and power your movement as you walk. These exercises can be obtained from a physiotherapist or a good sports therapist.

2 Plantar fasciitis

This can feel like anything from a dull ache to a sharp pulling feeling along the arch of the foot. Improper or worn shoes, over-pronation and high arches are common causes of plantar fasciitis. Depending on how severe your pain is, you won't necessarily need to stop walking. Avoid hills and wear supportive shoes that provide plenty of arch support and correct over-pronation. Calf stretches will help and you can rest and perhaps do other exercise such as swimming until you start to feel better.

3 Patellofemoral pain syndrome (PFPS)

This is commonly referred to as runner's knee, however it can affect walkers, especially if there are some hills en route. Weakness in the quadriceps and hips are the most common causes of this injury. Again rest is always a great response if you are suffering from this type of knee pain. It can be prevented by strengthening your quadriceps and hips but please make sure you seek help for any recurring injuries.

4 IT band syndrome (ITBS)

This can feel like a sharp pain on the outside of the knee but you may also feel a dull pain or tightness along the outside of the thigh or on the outer hip. Taking rest and strengthening your bottom muscles should resolve most cases. Icing the area will help reduce inflammation around the knee and stretching the hip is also recommended. If you have a foam roller use this along the thigh.

5 Achilles tendonitis

This can give you pain and swelling at the back of the heel. It can start as a dull ache but if you don't get it treated it could get worse. For mild cases, reducing how far you walk and sticking to flat, even surfaces will help along with ice to help inflammation. For more severe cases, rest and see a physiotherapist and go swimming and cycling until you feel better.

cell regeneration

Treating people, not patients.
Visit www.mbst-therapy.co.uk
or read treatment stories on Facebook: @mbstUK

Cell Regeneration and Clare House Physiotherapy, Casterton Lane, Tinwell PE9 3UQ
T: 01780 238 084   E: info@mbst-therapy.co.uk

MBST

1-2 HOUR WALKS

If you are looking for somewhere a bit different for a weekend stroll with the family and dogs you should find a bit of inspiration here. And they are certainly long enough to justify a refreshment at the end.

130 082132
Tally

8. Braceborough, Greatford and Shillingthorpe

Step back in time with this stroll to peaceful Shillingthorpe

THE ROUTE

Park in Braceborough down by the Old Hall which is a care home now. This is also the dead end lane that leads to the church and it's a very quiet part of this already peaceful little village.

Take the footpath in the south east corner of what looks like a village green and follow it south east across the fields to Greatford. Walk towards the village centre along the road for 100 metres and take the right turn footpath into Greatford Gardens. Follow the road with the church and the West Glen river on your left hand side. Keep going until you pick up the footpath leading out of the village down the left hand side of a house.

The path now runs through the woods behind Greatford Hall for 400 yards and, while you can't see much of this stunning old house, you get the idea of the scale of the gardens. At the end of the woods it's a right turn and then up a slight incline before turning left and crossing a couple of fields on the way up to Shillingthorpe. There used to be a big house in this

now deserted old park and woodland, but it was pulled down after the Second World War when it served as a convalescence home. The parkland is now used mainly for cattle grazing but the walls of the old garden remain, along with a few ruins which have been enveloped by greenery over the years.

It's a peaceful spot with some sad echoes of former glories but definitely worth a wander. But for this walk the path will bring you on to the main track which runs through the woodland and here you take a right and then very shortly afterwards bear right to head north. You will pass Banthorpe Wood on your left and then head north east on the path with wide open views over the Fens out to the east. On a clear day you can see a long way from here and you will feel like you are on the last piece of elevated land before mainland Europe, and you probably are.

This path leads down to the Greatford to Carlby road which you cross and then walk along the road back into Braceborough.

POINT OF INTEREST

Shillingthorpe Hall was built in 1796 possibly as an extension for the famous lunatic asylum at Greatford Hall run by Dr Willis of Madness of King George fame. It was also used as a private residence and for military purposes before its demise in 1953.

Braceborough

S/F

Shillingthorpe park

Greatford

ESSENTIAL INFORMATION

Difficulty rating

This is a very easy going walk with hardly any stiles.

Where to park
In Braceborough down by the Old Hall and the church.

Distance and time
Three and a half miles/ one hour 15 minutes.

Highlights
Braceborough and Greatford are both attractive villages and Shillingthorpe is a peaceful old park with some echoes of its grand past.

The pooch perspective
Plenty of opportunity for a good run and if it's a hot day you can get down to the West Glen river in Shillingthorpe Park for a cool off.

9. Elton and Fotheringhay
An historic, beautiful and perfectly English walk

THE ROUTE

This circular route has two obvious start points. You can either park in Elton and aim to stop at the Falcon in Fotheringhay for a drink on the way round, or start in Fotheringhay and aim to stop at the Crown in Elton on the way round. I have done it both ways and they both work well, but for this guide I will start in Elton. Park anywhere around Middle Street or the Crown. For the anti-clockwise route, make sure you take the footpath leading directly off Stocks Green (not the one down Chapel Lane).

You will know you are on the right path because it very quickly takes you past the mill and then the majestic river Nene as it sweeps through the Northamptonshire countryside. Cross the river and turn right immediately. There is a good spot for the dogs to cool off and have a drink right here. Then go over the smaller footbridge and turn left immediately.

Head west out over the flat field and when you get to the dismantled railway take the path which runs south west towards Middle Lodge. It's very clearly marked through the field. After two fields you will come to Middle Lodge, an isolated farmstead. Take the left hand route all around the farm buildings and pick up the path again on the other side. After another two fields you will reach Fotheringhay Road just 500 yards north of the village.

Walk down the road enjoying the impressive view of the church. If you want a drink at the Falcon turn right at the T-junction and it's just down the road on the left. If not then turn left at the T-junction and when you get to the big right hand turn pick up the Nene Way footpath straight ahead.

After passing through a farm you will find the old site of the motte & bailey castle on your right. As the site of Mary Queen of Scots' execution in February 1587 it's an integral part of British history and an interesting staging post on the walk. But once you've had your history lesson return to the Nene Way and strike out south east up and over a gentle undulation, through some arable crops and past the dismantled railway again. You will eventually come to a sheep pasture and then a lock on the river Nene. Cross the river and continue along the Nene Way. You will see plenty of long boats moored up on a sidewater and the path then goes around Warmington Mill.

Once you get past the mill make sure you take the left turn before the Nene Way goes underneath the A605. From here the footpath runs alongside a raised section of the main road for 400 yards but it's totally segregated so feels both safe and reasonably quiet. You soon come to a left turn and a track, which traverses a bank above a long strip of woodland heading north. You will eventually come to a gateway which leads straight into the southern section of Elton Park. Keep following the path and enjoying the splendid views until you come into the village on Chapel Lane.

ESSENTIAL INFORMATION

Difficulty rating

It's five miles but good underfoot and not many contours.

Where to park
For this version of the walk park somewhere near the Crown in Elton. If you want to finish in Fotheringhay then anywhere on the road near the Falcon will be fine.

Distance and time
Five miles, an hour and 40 minutes (it's pretty flat).

Highlights
Two lovely pubs and villages, Fotheringhay church and castle, the river Nene, and the beautiful English countryside.

The pooch perspective
A couple of good cooling off spots in the Nene, dog friendly sections in both pubs, hardly any livestock.

POINT OF INTEREST

Richard III was born at Fotheringhay Castle in 1452. Henry VIII gave the castle to his Queen, Katherine of Aragon. After their divorce it passed to each of his wives in succession. After the execution of Mary Queen of Scots in 1587 it was sold and eventually dismantled in 1628. Stone removed from the castle was used to build the Talbot Hotel in Oundle.

Reeland.
909 045

10. Lyndon and Wing

Step away from the hustle of modern life with a walk across the Chater valley from peaceful Lyndon to nearby Wing

THE ROUTE

Despite being little more than a couple of decent golf shots from the south shore of Rutland Water tiny Lyndon has retained its serene sense of detachment from the modern world. This is a direct result of most of the village remaining in possession of the Lyndon estate, and it makes it a perfect spot for a calming walk away from the worries of modern life.

Park anywhere in the village, but near St Martin's church is as good a place as any, and set out north-west along the Manton road. This is not a busy thoroughfare so enjoy the ancient woodland. Very shortly before the road reaches the main road along the south shore of Rutland Water there is a footpath to the left. Take this path and head downhill with a bank of trees on your left. Don't be surprised if you see a few pheasants roaming around and a gamekeeper or two.

When you reach the valley bottom and the pretty river Chater carry on south over the river, across the railway and up the hill to Wing. When you get to the road on the edge of the village turn right and walk to the King's Arms. This is a welcoming pub which does excellent food if you have built in time for lunch. But even if you are not eating, go and have a drink. You won't regret it.

To return to Lyndon walk down Middle Street or Church Street in Wing and you will find another footpath which takes you back down to the railway and then the same bridge over the Chater that you crossed on the way out. After you cross the bridge turn right and head north east back across the hillside towards Lyndon. You will enter the village along the south side of grand old Lyndon Hall, which was completed in 1677.

Once you are back in the village savour the tranquil atmosphere of a community which has not succumbed to detrimental levels of development, and offers a glimpse of a bygone country life. The only downside with this walk is that it may leave you feeling a little envious of the lucky people who get to live in this rural paradise.

POINT OF INTEREST

Lyndon Hall dates back to 1671 and the village has benefitted from the protective ownership of just two families since then.

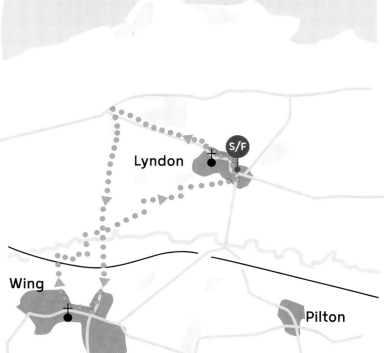

Lyndon

S/F

Wing

Pilton

ESSENTIAL INFORMATION

Difficulty rating

Where to park
There is plenty of room near the church in Lyndon.

Distance and time
Four miles/an hour and 20 minutes.

Highlights
The peaceful atmosphere of Lyndon which has been protected from over-development and beautiful Wing. Lovely views over the Chater Valley and the little river itself.

The pooch perspective
This walk is pretty dog-friendly, with a nice river.

11. Market Overton and Edmondthorpe

This north Rutland stroll offers wide reaching views of half the county and two very different but equally charming villages

THE ROUTE

Park opposite the Black Bull on Teigh Road in under-rated Market Overton and the start of the walk is immediately opposite down the lane just before the church. After about 150 yards you will come to a footpath junction where you can choose to do this loop clockwise or anti-clockwise. I chose the latter so carried straight on across the top of the ridge offering far-reaching views of the Vale of Catmose to the south and west. But make sure you aren't too distracted by the view to follow the path as it bears left into the field here, rather than carrying along the track.

That's what I did and it took me a while to work out where I had gone wrong. Assuming you do spot the path though you will soon come up to the corner of the woodland, crossing the county boundary into Leicestershire as you do. Carry straight on with the wood on your left until you get to the next corner. Turn left here over the stile and into the wood.

Even on a hot day in July this path was more than a bit boggy, courtesy of hoof prints, so walking boots are definitely a good idea. The path soon comes out of the wood and the track meanders down and around Hall Farm on the way to Edmondthorpe. This is a conservation area given over to the encouragement of ground nesting birds so if you have got the dog with you then please keep it under close control during the nesting season (late spring and early summer).

You will come out on to Woodwell Head Lane where it's a left turn and then follow the road up to Main Street in Edmondthorpe, an almost untouched estate village which has retained a tremendous amount of its idyllic rural charm. Turn left and pass the Village Social Club, which must be a contender for most aesthetically pleasing social club in the country. There is a return path shortly after, which I chose not to take because it runs very close to the outward path but it's another option.

I stayed on the road past the church and took the path to the left through the farmyard. Follow the footpath down over a little stream and through three gates, which were surrounded by overgrown vegetation when I went through. Join the road for 100 yards until you get to The Lodge where there is a footpath heading east back towards Market Overton. From here it's a pretty straight uphill path, with glimpses of Edmondthorpe Hall to the left, but there are a few different paths so take your pick. It's hard to get lost when you can see the target ahead.

ESSENTIAL INFORMATION

Difficulty rating

Where to park
Opposite the Black Bull in Market Overton.

Distance and time
Four and three quarter miles/An hour and 45 minutes.

Highlights
Far reaching views to the west over the Vale of Catmose. Untouched Edmondthorpe. Market Overton has a surprisingly grand village centre and the Black Bull is a cracking pub.

The pooch perspective
A shortage of water on a hot summer's day might be a problem and the ground nesting bird conservation area means control is essential. In truth it probably won't be your dog's favourite walk but it's still worth it.

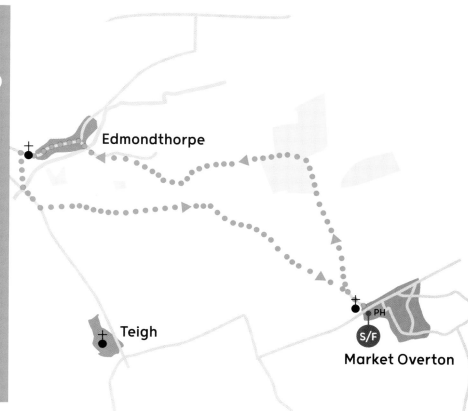

Edmondthorpe

Teigh

Market Overton
PH
S/F

Barrow

POINT OF INTEREST

Market Overton is almost on the western boundary of Kendrew Barracks, which was RAF Cottesmore until April 2012. As an RAF base it was home to the Tri-National Tornado Training Establishment, involving the UK, Germany and Italy, and latterly it was a harrier base.

915025 Rutland

12. Pilton and the Luffenhams

Rutland Water might be just over the hill, but it's hard to tell on this tranquil ramble

THE ROUTE

I parked on the verge near the crossroads at Pilton, but you could just as easily start and finish this walk in South or North Luffenham, perhaps with a view to walking straight to a pub at the end. There is no pub in tiny Pilton.

Walk east out of the village on Pilton road and after 200 yards you will see the bridleway ahead as the road bends to the left. Take the bridleway and keep to it as it goes gently uphill and then turns to the left along a hedge-lined route in an almost straight line for more than a mile to South Luffenham.

You will get some good views of North Luffenham church on your left and the hedgerow and occasional spinney offer good protection from the wind on this exposed piece of high ground. On the way you will cross over Glebe Road which connects Morcott and North Luffenham, but keep going straight ahead and you will descend into South Luffenham across an open arable field.

When you get into the village turn left as soon as you hit the road and keep going along North Luffenham Road as it leaves the village and then curves to the right and downhill. You will go under the railway bridge and then cross the stone bridge over the River Chater. The dogs can cool off and have a drink here if necessary. Almost immediately after the bridge there is a metal kissing gate in the hedgerow on the left. Go through this and follow the path as it goes uphill through pastures towards North Luffenham.

You will arrive in North Luffenham through an iron gate and then follow the road round to the left until you come to the lane down to the school and the church. Walk down here and pick up the footpath on the south west corner of the church. This path leads out diagonally over the sheep pasture and the River Chater until you come out on Glebe Road. Walk south over the railway bridge and then turn right when you come to the crossroads and go past Heathcote Cottages. From here it's just less than one mile along this pretty country lane back to Pilton.

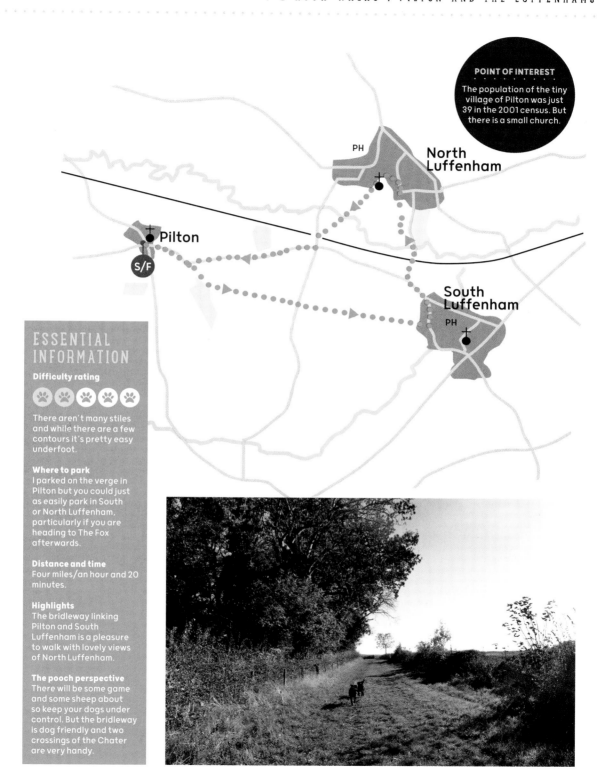

POINT OF INTEREST

The population of the tiny village of Pilton was just 39 in the 2001 census. But there is a small church.

North Luffenham

PH

Pilton

S/F

South Luffenham

PH

ESSENTIAL INFORMATION

Difficulty rating

There aren't many stiles and while there are a few contours it's pretty easy underfoot.

Where to park
I parked on the verge in Pilton but you could just as easily park in South or North Luffenham, particularly if you are heading to The Fox afterwards.

Distance and time
Four miles/an hour and 20 minutes.

Highlights
The bridleway linking Pilton and South Luffenham is a pleasure to walk with lovely views of North Luffenham.

The pooch perspective
There will be some game and some sheep about so keep your dogs under control. But the bridleway is dog friendly and two crossings of the Chater are very handy.

13. Seaton and Morcott

Make the most of Rutland's contours with this panoramic loop back to pretty little Seaton

THE ROUTE

Park near the George & Dragon pub in Seaton. Take the Rutland Round footpath which heads along the road north east out of Seaton. This is a beautiful country lane with hardly any traffic and some great views to the south. After about one kilometre you will come to a right hand bend in the road and see the footpath continuing straight on. Take the footpath straight down the hill along the field margin. At the bottom you will cross the old disused railway line and then go across a wooden bridge over a stream which is a convenient refreshment spot for the dogs.

After the bridge the path goes straight on over the field in front to pick up the hedgeline and then the very obvious path heading slightly north east uphill towards the A47. When you get near the main road don't forget to turn and appreciate the view to the south, before crossing to The Cockpit and then taking the footpath on the right.

This will take you gently downhill across a couple of fields and into Morcott via Mount Pleasant Road. Turn right on the High Street and walk to the junction with the A6121. Turn right again and then take care crossing the A47 before heading up the B672 just before the petrol station. It sounds like a lot of crossing of busy roads but it's a very minor inconvenience.

Walk up the B672 for 500m and then when the road turns sharp left keep going straight on to the bridleway.

This very attractive tree-lined route gently drops down towards the Welland Valley offering superb views all around and is something of a hidden gem. At the end of the bridleway join the road for 200m before taking the right turn on to the quiet road back to Seaton. This climbs uphill gradually and goes over one railway bridge before bringing you back on to the Rutland Round and then it's straight back to Seaton.

ESSENTIAL INFORMATION

Difficulty rating

There is nothing difficult but there are a few steep climbs.

Where to park
Either park in the George & Dragon car park (if you are going to use it later) or somewhere nearby in Seaton.

Distance and time
Four and a quarter miles/ an hour and a half.

Highlights
Panoramic views of Harringworth Viaduct to the south from different points on the walk. Some lovely Rutland hills and the pretty bridleway on the way back.

The pooch perspective
The stream in the first half is well placed, otherwise there isn't much fresh water. There is no livestock but keep your dog under control because there will probably be plenty of game about.

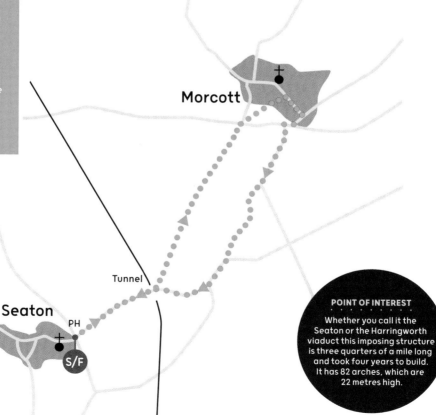

Morcott

Seaton

PH

S/F

Tunnel

POINT OF INTEREST

Whether you call it the Seaton or the Harringworth viaduct this imposing structure is three quarters of a mile long and took four years to build. It has 82 arches, which are 22 metres high.

14. Stamford and Easton-on-the-Hill

This classic walk incorporates town and country and never fails

THE ROUTE

Start on the town meadows in Stamford by Bath Row and head west towards the A1. Go through the gateway in the first fence and keep going over the meadows for half a mile until you get to Broadeng Bridge (the green steel monstrosity) over the Welland. Cross the bridge and turn right. Keep the river on your right for 250 yards and then bear left towards an underpass beneath the A1. If you get to the weir you have gone too far.

Once you have passed under the A1 the path takes you up to a pedestrian railway crossing and away from the traffic noise. After this you know you have left Lincolnshire because there are real contours. Seasoned Fen-hoppers will find the ascent to Easton reasonably demanding but hardier Rutlanders should positively skip up the slope.

In due course the footpath, which is part of the Jurassic and Macmillan Ways, brings you right into the stunning old part of Easton-on-the-Hill. Head down Church Street

into the village with the church on your right and enjoy this wonderful example of a stone-built English village at its very best.

When you reach the T-junction in the middle of the village you will find the Blue Bell pub on your right, which is a good spot for a drink. If you aren't stopping, turn left and walk through the dip in the road before joining the A43 for less than 100 yards and then take care crossing the busy road to take the footpath which cuts off diagonally on the south side of the A43. Head down here for half a mile through some arable fields and pretty woodland until you come to the Wothorpe ruins.

Here you can either turn left and follow the footpath which wends its way back down under the A1 and through wealthy Wothorpe to Stamford, or stay on the track as it heads over the A1. The latter route is flanked by some glorious horse chestnut trees and brings you out by Burghley Golf Course where you turn left and walk the half mile or so down the hill into Stamford.

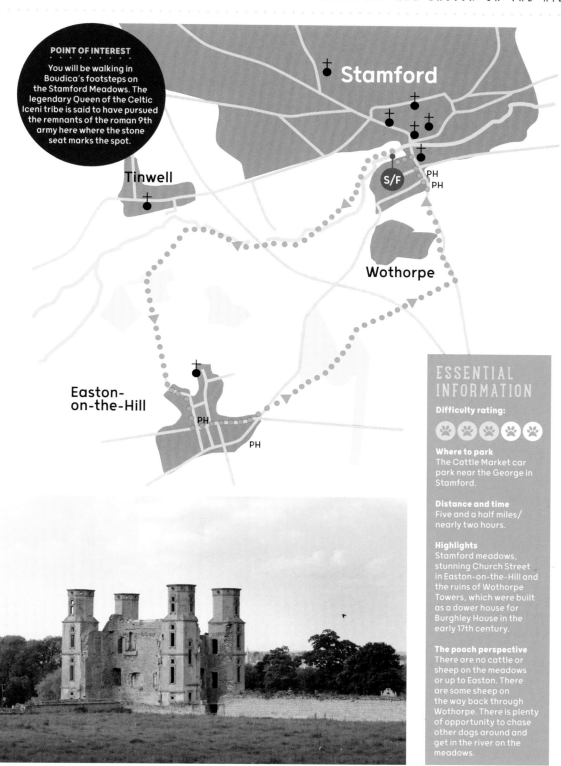

POINT OF INTEREST

You will be walking in Boudica's footsteps on the Stamford Meadows. The legendary Queen of the Celtic Iceni tribe is said to have pursued the remnants of the roman 9th army here where the stone seat marks the spot.

Stamford

Tinwell

S/F

PH
PH

Wothorpe

Easton-on-the-Hill

PH

PH

ESSENTIAL INFORMATION

Difficulty rating:

🐾 🐾 🐾 🐾 🐾

Where to park
The Cattle Market car park near the George in Stamford.

Distance and time
Five and a half miles/ nearly two hours.

Highlights
Stamford meadows, stunning Church Street in Easton-on-the-Hill and the ruins of Wothorpe Towers, which were built as a dower house for Burghley House in the early 17th century.

The pooch perspective
There are no cattle or sheep on the meadows or up to Easton. There are some sheep on the way back through Wothorpe. There is plenty of opportunity to chase other dogs around and get in the river on the meadows.

2+ HOUR WALKS

These are really designed for when you want a proper leg stretch in the open countryside, and with some of the hills in Rutland they shouldn't be under-estimated.

15. Belton-in-Rutland and Ridlington

If you are after some undulations then you will definitely find them in this pretty corner of Rutland

THE ROUTE

Park somewhere around the church or on Chapel Street in Belton and head downhill and north out of the village on Lambley Lodge Lane or Leighfield Way as it is also known. After about 100 metres you will see the footpath sign to the right heading into the grassy field on a slope. Follow the clear markers over the stream where the dogs can paddle if they wish and then go up the first hill, which provides a nice view of Belton behind you from the top. Drop down the other side and curve around to the left before heading up hill number two.

When I did this walk there was no marker at the bottom but it's pretty clear where to go up the track. It's a steep climb (as will be obvious from one glance at the contour lines on the OS Map) and will get your heart working hard. At Park Farm at the top turn left and quick right again to head down a 500 metre farm track with a wonderful newly laid hedge on the right. At the end of the hedge turn left and follow the field edge around to get to Holygate Road.

Turn right and walk into Ridlington with views of Rutland Water to the north east. Go past some large houses on your left in Ridlington and when the road turns right you will see the bridleway ahead on the next left hand bend. Head down here but take the right turn after 100 metres. Follow the signs and head downhill, through some woodland and then up the third climb of this walk on what was a very muddy track when I was there. When you come to the top stay alert and make sure you take the right hand branch at the next footpath junction. There are superb views to the west from the top of this stretch so take a moment to enjoy them before the descent.

After a long straight path it's a slight right hand turn and then the route takes a left curve before a left turn up hill four. When you get to the top of this one you will be able to see Belton again, but head straight downhill towards the layby on the A47 and turn right 200 metres before the main road to take the attractive path and last but not least hill back into beautiful little Belton with its stunning ironstone houses.

POINT OF INTEREST

Architectural historian Sir Nikolaus Pevsner said of Belton-in-Rutland: "The village round the church is delightful. Its highlights are the row of ironstone cottages with mullioned windows south-east of the church and a group further north, especially Hillcrest, and west of the church two individual houses, the Old Hall and Westbourne House."

Ridlington

Belton-in-Rutland

S/F

Allexton

Wardley

ESSENTIAL INFORMATION

Difficulty rating

Four paws, it's hilly.

Where to park
Near the church or on Chapel Street in Belton in Rutland.

Distance and time
Five and a quarter miles/ two hours (at least).

Highlights
Lots of lovely hills to get your heart rate up and provide great views of the surrounding countryside. Belton and Ridlington are both beautiful and peaceful Rutland villages.

The pooch perspective
A couple of streams on the way round for cooling off and not a lot of livestock so your dogs will enjoy this one too.

16. Exton Park and Fort Henry

With plenty of well-established estate roads and few stiles this is a good walk for a wet day

THE ROUTE

I parked on Pudding Bag Lane in Exton but it doesn't really matter where you park as it's a circular route. Head to the large collection of Exton estate farm buildings on the north west corner of the village. Follow the footpath through one gate and then keep heading north west on a long straight estate road. You will soon go through a belt of trees and then take the right hand turn to follow the path as it curves around the northern edge of this belt.

Turn left at the next footpath/road junction and head north east keeping Tunneley Wood on your right hand side. This stretch is part of the Viking Way. It's easy walking on these estate roads and you will more than likely see a few other people out and about because it's attractive old parkland and great for exercise. When you reach the top end of Tunneley Wood turn left on the Viking Way and after 500m of undulating terrain turn right and head east on a long exposed 2km stretch.

You will eventually come into Osprey Wood and see the path dropping down to the right off the track. Take this path and follow it round past Fort Henry Lake and the fort on the far bank (actually a boathouse which must have been perfect for Edwardian summer parties).

Keep heading south with Lower Lake on your right and then turn right when you reach the bottom of this smaller stretch of ornamental water. After one kilometre turn left and enjoy the climb before Exton hoves into view again. From here it's a very straight run back into the village with the church dead ahead all the way.

POINT OF INTEREST

The present Exton Hall is the private home of the Noel family and was built in the 19th century close to the ruins of the original house. In 1869 a Roman Catholic chapel, dedicated to St Thomas of Canterbury was added.

Exton

PH

S/F

ESSENTIAL INFORMATION

Difficulty rating

It's good underfoot and should be suitable for most people but it is exposed.

Where to park
Anywhere in the old part of the village but I chose Pudding Bag Lane because it's near the farm at the start of the walk.

Distance and time
Five and a half miles/ two hours.

Highlights
Exton is an attractive village, the ancient parkland is well laid out and Fort Henry is a good landmark.

The pooch perspective
It's arable farmland mostly but there are sheep fields nearer the village.

17. King's Cliffe, Blatherwycke and Fineshade

A long walk of three distinctly different parts whch works in every sense

THE ROUTE

As with all circular routes there are a number of parking options, but I chose to park on the very western edge of King's Ciffe, where West Street meets Blatherwycke Road. You could park in Blatherwycke or at Fineshade but I felt this worked quite well for me and the dogs. Head south down Orchard Lane and turn right after a minute to take the path which skirts across the bottom edge of the allotments. Once you clear the allotments the path heads out into open grass fields and soon crosses the Willow Brook, which it then essentially tracks (with a few deviations) for a mile until you reach Blatherwycke Lake.

You will go through Alders Farm on the way and you will need to keep the dogs under close control from this point because there is a lot of game in the area. A couple of field boundaries after Alders Farm you will notice the landscape changing from pasture land to manicured parkland and large arable fields with well planted copses on hilltops. The path goes gradually uphill along the southern shore of Blatherwycke Lake and ultimately brings you into this tiny village around the back of the church and a grand but rather derelict looking old building.

When you get to the road in the village turn right and walk down over the picturesque bridge and then up the hill on the other side. Follow the road round to the right and, with the lake on your right hand side, you will soon come to the footpath which heads out north towards Fineshade from a road junction. Keep following the path as it starts to gradually climb towards the woods in the distance. Just before the path goes around the south western fringe of the woods it starts to drop downhill quickly and at the bottom there is a fourway footpath junction where you keep going straight. You are now also on the Jurassic Way as it winds its way from Banbury to Stamford.

Go up the steep bank and firstly you will have good views of Fineshade Abbey on the left and you will then pass another magnificent house with its own lake. Keep following the path until you reach the road into Fineshade Top Lodge. Turn right here and when you get to the Lodge there is a very handy outside tap and water bowl for the dogs in a corner of the courtyard. There's also a café and toilets should you need them. But don't go any further in that direction because the Jurassic Way carries on past the front of the Top Lodge and then heads off on a woodland road initially to the south and then curving around to the east.

From Top Lodge it's nearly two miles back to King's Cliffe but most of that is along the metalled road in Westhay Wood. Near the end of the wood you leave the Jurassic Way behind when it heads north. Carry on west through a yard and then take Wood Lane south back into King's Cliffe.

ESSENTIAL INFORMATION

Difficulty rating

This is quite a long walk and there are plenty of undulations.

Where to park
I parked on the western edge of King's Cliffe where West Street meets Blatherwycke Road but you can park in Blatherwycke or at Fineshade Top Lodge (pay & display).

Distance and time
Six and a half miles/two and a quarter hours.

Highlights
The first section along the Willow Brook is straight out of Enid Blyton. The area around Blatherwycke bears all the hallmarks of affluence and the lake and village are both very attractive. Fineshade Abbey and the woods are then totally different again.

The pooch perspective
Brilliant by the Willow Brook but restricted around Blatherwycke. And it's good for the dogs in the woods.

King's Cliffe

S/F

Blatherwycke

POINT OF INTEREST

What is known today as Fineshade Abbey was originally a Norman castle, then an Augustinian priory which was converted to a residence and then replaced by a country house. That building was demolished in 1956 and today the converted stable block makes for an excellent landmark on the Jurassic Way.

18. Stamford and Uffington

Stamford's finest example of Norman architecture, St Leonard's Priory, is a beautiful waypoint on this urban and rural ramble

THE ROUTE

If you are coming from the centre of Stamford then you will need to navigate to St Leonard's Priory at the eastern end of Priory Road just before the Morrisons roundabout. Once you have enjoyed the atmosphere around the ancient priory, walk east across the south side of the Morrisons roundabout and past the empty garage before taking the track down to Hudd's Mill on the right. Turn left at the bottom and then turn right to cross over the first wooden bridge over the millstream. Cross over the main course of the Welland over another bridge. Head straight on and through the kissing gate approaching the railway, but turn left on to the path in the woods before you get to the railway.

From here stay on the track, which is also the Torpel Way, for a mile. As you walk down this peaceful natural corridor, with the trees meeting overhead, you will also see the Woodland Welcome signs on your left. This means the owner permits people to go and wander around the newly planted woodland down by the river.

You will eventually reach the road just south of the stone bridge over the Welland. Cross the bridge and walk up the hill in to Uffington. (There is a parallel path which

runs north of the river back to Hudds Mill which makes this a nice loop for another day).

Walk through the village on the pavement by the side of the main road, but make sure you stop at the wonderful Bertie Arms for refreshment on the way if you have time.

After the Bertie Arms walk west almost all the way out of the village in the Stamford direction and, just after the layby on the right, you will see the footpath sign pointing down a track to the right. Take this path over some exposed farmland with great views all around for a good mile before the path turns left and heads west towards Cobbs Nook Farm on the Newstead Road. Follow the path around the field edges and when you reach the bridleway turn left and then straight on to Newstead Road for 100 yards. Then turn right and over the stile in the hedgerow to bring you on to the meadows with stunning views over Stamford beyond. You are now on the Macmillan Way and you will follow it downhill and south west over the River Gwash and beyond, until you reach a track which heads up on to Ryhall Road. Turn left at the top of the track and this will take you back into Stamford town centre, although there is a path behind Morrisons just after Homebase if your car is there.

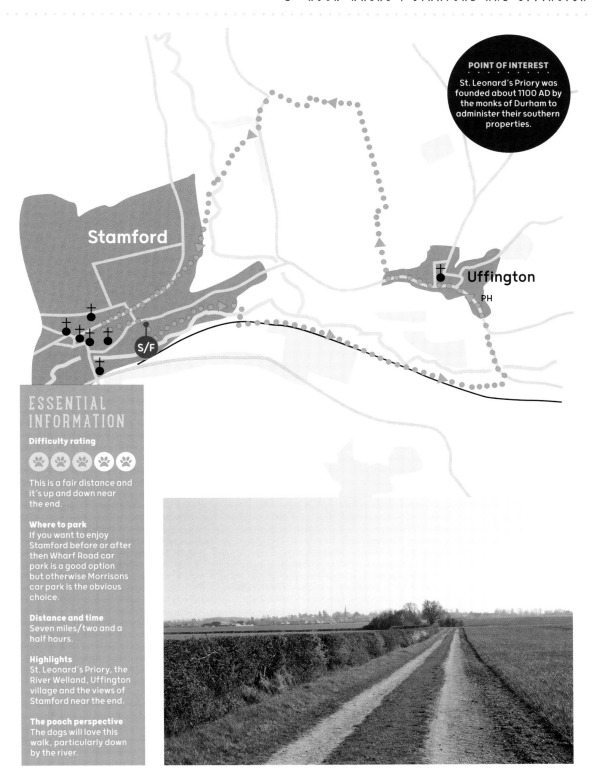

POINT OF INTEREST

St. Leonard's Priory was founded about 1100 AD by the monks of Durham to administer their southern properties.

Stamford

Uffington

PH

ESSENTIAL INFORMATION

Difficulty rating

This is a fair distance and it's up and down near the end.

Where to park
If you want to enjoy Stamford before or after then Wharf Road car park is a good option but otherwise Morrisons car park is the obvious choice.

Distance and time
Seven miles/two and a half hours.

Highlights
St. Leonard's Priory, the River Welland, Uffington village and the views of Stamford near the end.

The pooch perspective
The dogs will love this walk, particularly down by the river.

19. The Witham Five

This loop takes in five villages, an ancient oak tree, a golf course and a once famous spa, all in just eight miles

THE ROUTE

You can park near to the church on the main road in Witham. Take the footpath to the left of the church and set off north. You will soon cross the bridge over the small brook and head uphill on a narrow track alongside a house. Turn right on to the track at the top and go past the Grange, a lavish looking new build on your right. You will soon see the footpath sign to the left, so head off into the field and make sure you make the right turn in the direction of Toft after 200 yards.

This path then goes through three fields as it gradually descends towards the A6121 Bourne Road. When you get to the road turn left and take care walking over the hump back bridge on the way into Toft. At the Golf Course

turn right at the footpath sign and turn right again to go past the front of the shop. The footpath south through the course is clearly marked, but I would advise caution because you may be in the landing zone sometimes. Follow the signs and you will go through a hedge and see the sign for the path to Manthorpe across the field. Head south east and you will soon be on the lane into Manthorpe.

Turn right to walk almost all the way through the village and you will find the footpath again on your left just before the end of the village. Take this path downhill and head for the bridge over the river just north of Bowthorpe Park Farm. The stile here was basically non-existent when I did this walk, but you can still get over the fence and cross the bridge. Then go straight uphill to the farm where the gate is attached by a flimsy piece of string. Turn left after the gate and then immediate right to pick up the path as it goes diagonally through an enclosed field. If you look to your right here you will see the Bowthorpe Oak tree which, at more than 1,000 years old, may be the oldest oak in England.

After the next stile turn right and after about 400 yards turn right over the bridge and then take the path which heads across the field south to Spa Lodge Farm. It's not very clearly cut in the field but you can see the post you are aiming for on the corner in the distance. When you get to Spa Lodge Farm walk the track down past Station House and continue south east until you get to Braceborough.

When you get to the village turn right and look out for the footpath sign on the right. After the small stream take the right hand option and head across the fields past Braceborough Lodge and into Braceborough Woods. Do a very quick right/left when you get to the woods and you will be on the clearly marked path which leads out into the open fields all the way to the A6121 and Carlby just about a mile away. Cross the main road and then take the road into Carlby.

Walk almost all the way through the village (ignoring one footpath sign on your right) and then just before you come to the edge of Carlby take the footpath which goes up between two houses. It's hard to see until you are on it but you have to take this path. It winds around behind the back of some houses before straightening out and heading north. From here it's a beautiful path for a mile and a half all the way back to Witham.

ESSENTIAL INFORMATION

Difficulty rating

It's eight miles but apart from a few tricky stiles it's fairly good underfoot.

Where to park
Near the church on the main road in Witham.

Distance and time
Eight miles/two hours and 40 minutes.

Highlights
The massive and ancient Bowthorpe Oak, the tranquility of Braceborough Spa and Braceborough Woods, and the path from Carlby to Witham.

The pooch perspective
The route does cross a few streams but some of them may run dry in high summer. And I encountered livestock between Manthorpe and Bowthorpe Park Farm but nowhere else.

Toft

S/F

PH

Witham on the Hill

Manthorpe

POINT OF INTEREST

Braceborough Spa, rising in the grounds of Spa House, was a popular retreat because of its natural spring waters. A bathhouse was built in 1841 and Dr Willis treated George III here for his so called 'madness'. The King supposedly stayed in a wing of nearby Shillingthorpe Hall, now demolished, and there is a tablet in Greatford Church commemorating his stay. There was a stop at Braceborough Spa Halt on the Essendine to Bourne railway but the spa closed in 1939.

Carlby

Braceborough

20. Uppingham, Lyddington, Seaton and Bisbrooke

This superb route includes a market town, three villages and plenty of hills

THE ROUTE

For this guide I will recommend starting in Uppingham and taking the anti-clockwise option but the choice is yours. Park near the cricket pavilion on Seaton Road, walk up High Street East and and take the alleyway which runs south a few doors down from the Lake Isle hotel and restaurant. Cross South View road and the path then goes through a couple of big dippers as it leaves the town behind. In wet conditions this is probably the trickiest part of the walk because the hills are steep and muddy. But it should get your heart rate going nice and early on a cold day. After the two dips the path crosses the playing fields of Uppingham Community College and over a quiet road before entering the open country looking down at Lyddington and beyond.

When you cross the stile at the bottom of the hill which brings you onto the road into Lyddington you have a choice. You can either stay on the road into the village and enjoy what is probably Rutland's most attractive settlement. Or if you are familiar with Lyddington and want to get cracking cross the road and take the field path which by-passes the village via a couple of paddocks with a pretty stream to the right.

Both routes are charming in their own way and both will bring you to the mile and a half long path to Seaton.

The path takes the low route with intriguing Prestley Hill and The Barrows to the right. With no roads in view it's a soothing experience as you gradually approach Seaton on its hillside perch.

Just below Seaton the path joins Grange Lane which heads up the hill and joins Seaton Road at the top. Turn right here and walk into the village. Look out for the stone steps on the left which lead to the footpath. If you need a refreshment stop then keep going until you get to the George & Dragon which is a good village pub.

But if not take the stone steps and follow the path up and over the hill. Once you are over the crest you can see Glaston and the A47 ahead, but the path bears downhill and to the left over the dismantled railway and towards Bisbrooke. After the old railway you will soon cross a clear stream on a wooden footbridge before crossing another stile on the approach to Bisbrooke. I think the best way to enter any village is via a footpath and it's no different with sleepy little Bisbrooke, as St John the Baptist church gently hoves into view.

Once you have passed the church carry on over the crossroads on to Bottom Road and pick up the path again as it leaves the village via The Inhams, a row of houses on the western edge. From here it's straight over a hilltop on an exposed path and back into Uppingham.

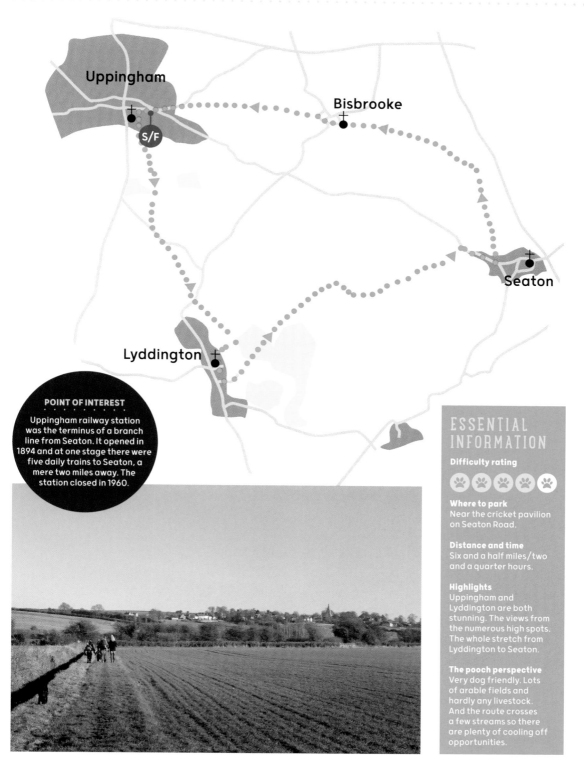

Uppingham

Bisbrooke

S/F

Seaton

Lyddington

POINT OF INTEREST

Uppingham railway station was the terminus of a branch line from Seaton. It opened in 1894 and at one stage there were five daily trains to Seaton, a mere two miles away. The station closed in 1960.

ESSENTIAL INFORMATION

Difficulty rating

Where to park
Near the cricket pavilion on Seaton Road.

Distance and time
Six and a half miles/two and a quarter hours.

Highlights
Uppingham and Lyddington are both stunning. The views from the numerous high spots. The whole stretch from Lyddington to Seaton.

The pooch perspective
Very dog friendly. Lots of arable fields and hardly any livestock. And the route crosses a few streams so there are plenty of cooling off opportunities.

21. West Deeping, Maxey and Market Deeping

A surprisingly rural route along the River Welland in Market Deeping makes this an unexpected gem

THE ROUTE

Park somewhere near the church in West Deeping, which must be one of the prettiest settings for a church in this part of the country. Having enjoyed this fine sight head south out of the village over the river bridge and turn left shortly after into a long meadow. Walk through the meadow and you will come to Maxey Mill in due course. Follow the path around the mill and when you come to the road you will see a path opposite heading into the Maxey Lakes area. Take this path and follow the route until you are in Maxey village proper. Find your way to the High Street (the main road through the village) and turn left to walk out towards Northborough.

Just before the last houses on the right hand side of the road the footpath heads out on the left hand side of the road across the fields towards Deeping Gate. Head out on this clearly marked path and you will soon come to the horse paddocks around Fox Cover Farm. Follow the signs and take care crossing the A15, then keep heading east, crossing Lincoln Road which was the old A15 and then come to Deeping St James Road. This first section is across flat arable land and, apart from the two roads, is surprisingly peaceful, featuring some typical fenland big

skies. When you get to Deeping St James Road turn left and carry on until you get to the bridge over the Welland in Deeping Gate.

Just before you get to the bridge, and unseen until you reach this point, there is a footpath off to the left. Take this path which runs all the way along the southern bank of the Welland as it passes through the Deepings. Initially you will have a row of attractive older houses on your left but after you pass Deeping High Locks it starts to open out and you will soon be in a more rural setting, even though Market Deeping is just over the river on the right. It's a surprisingly rural feel to a footpath which goes through the middle of a town. Keep following the path and you will re-cross the old main road just south of Market Deeping Bridge. I recommend you keep right and follow the path as it meanders along near the south bank of the Welland.

You will walk underneath the new A15 (graffiti alert) and will soon be treated to the idyllic view of the mill and gardens in another pleasantly unexpected feature of this walk. From the mill, keep the river on your right and head south west for a mile or so until you come out on Mill Road on the northern edge of Maxey. Turn right and retrace your steps to lovely West Deeping.

ESSENTIAL INFORMATION

Difficulty rating

It's flat and, provided it's not been raining too much, it's very easy under foot.

Where to park
Near the church in West Deeping or on the main road.

Distance and time
Six and a half miles/two and a quarter hours.

Highlights
The surprisingly rural route along the south bank of the Welland through Market Deeping. The water mill on the western edge of Deeping, Maxey Mill and some fenland big skies.

The pooch perspective
You won't see a lot of livestock on the way round and it's by the river for more than half the walk so your dogs will love it.

Deeping Gate

West Deeping

PH

S/F

Maxey

PH

POINT OF INTEREST

The River Welland which passes through Market Deeping is the Old Course of the river, with the bulk of the Welland actually flowing through the Maxey Cut, which runs to the south from Tallington to Peakirk, where the Old Course and the Maxey Cut reunite to form one course towards Crowland and Spalding.

5

of the finest villages

The area is packed with thriving communities of all sizes and this is just a small selection of the jewels in the crown

1 LYDDINGTON

A series of stunning ironstone houses, the ancient Bede House, a triangular village green and two good pubs make this linear village in the Welland valley a strong contender for best in Rutland.

2 UFFINGTON

An improbably grand old church, a thriving village pub and a strong sense of community make this little settlement right on the eastern edge of Stamford one of the area's most sought after villages.

3 EMPINGHAM

Right in the heart of Rutland and just beyond the eastern shore of the eponymous man-made piece of water, Main Street boasts a parade of pretty houses and the walk down to the North Brook is a pleasure in itself.

4 BARROWDEN

Classically formed around the village green and adjacent duck pond this is considered one of the most quintessentially English villages in the area.

5 TEIGH

This is the Joker in the pack because it's so small and has no pub; but it's very pretty. And its status as one of only 53 'Thankful Villages', one which saw all its members of the Armed Forces return alive from the First World War, is scarily educational for what it reveals about the impact of that conflict on our nation.